The Fun and Happy Depression

Jay Ocean

Published by THEM BOIS Books, 2020.

THE FUN AND HAPPY DEPRESSION

First edition. September 17, 2020.

ISBN: 978-1393214670

Written by Jay Ocean.

Table of Contents

Blackout Poem 1

Dedicated to my mother.

Mary's Rose

Even though Mary's Rose was sweet and sour,

She was also quite a liar.

Her mood couldn't get any higher.

One day Mary got very bitter and vile,

All her friends turned and ran another mile.

They said that she wasn't worthwhile.

All of a sudden Mary thought that she was rich,

One might even say that she was quite a lich.

Everyone in town would hope she would get sick.

When Mary lost her rose, she became very distraught.

So much so by the fact she lost everything she got.

THE FUN AND HAPPY DEPRESSION

Royalty

Say hi to your new life

And Hopefully, you won't take it for granted.

Shallow waters lay down and lie

While I have to get what's rightfully mine.

Quit lying, you know that you want this life.

I tried to save you from lying to yourself

about your love for our new life.

BoJack

We all have a little BoJack in use.

Yes, we do.

The kind that we all regret.

Yes, we do.

Our life is dedicated to the opposite.

Yes, it is.

We drive the good away and attract the bad.

Yes, I do.

Magnum Opus

Take my career out this day

If I had friends, I'd treat them in the worst way.

Most will help me on a cold day

All I wanted to do was help my ex friend Trey.

Help me start my career off with a hit

So that I can make what I see fit.

You say that you help save souls that I see in the dirty grit,

It's about dang time for us to have a hit.

THE FUN AND HAPPY DEPRESSION

Judge

Judge by the ways we talk.

Judge by the way walk.

Judge by the way we sulk.

Judge by the way we rock.

Eventually, we all get Sentenced to an eternity in forever grace.

The best part is when we get to break the spell.

F.A.M.E.E.

A man walks in me

I wonder heaven

I hear echos

I see black

I want to love and fame

I am man

I pretend to be happy

I feel flight

I touch wind

I worry about death

I cry about love

I am man

I understand

I say bye

I dream big

I try to fail

I hope to fly

I am man

THE FUN AND HAPPY DEPRESSION

Paranormal Affair

Why do all the beautiful ones come at a great cost?

That's what we all wonder inside.

Why must they always leave us with the feeble hearts?

To this day, I can't believe that they used to be fine.

Even with the fact that I was already entangled

They still came right for my still beating heart.

Why must it come to this conclusion?

Who knows why this love came from a farce?

FROM A BOX
1777
FOLK ART OF RURAL PENNSYLVANIA PLATE No. 1
INDEX OF AMERICAN DESIGN PENNA ART PROJECT W P A

Aladdin

Help me slay pirates that cause crime and sorrow

While I live this life forever and ever.

Just like Aladdin.

Just like Aladdin.

They can't fire me from this life that we live and strive in

And give love to our fellow homies and fallen brothers.

Just like Aladdin.

Just like Aladdin.

THE FUN AND HAPPY DEPRESSION

Wednesday

The way their hair moves in the shining moonlight

It makes my insides feel all warm and fuzzy on a summer's day.

Their 5'10 height only bothers the weak and frail

I can't wait to swim with her on this bright Wednesday day.

The loving doesn't ever stop at the beach when they are around

While drinking cool Vanilla Fil-A.

My love for this day just doesn't stop moving and flowing

Even with the sour days, I had in May.

Space

An alien she shares

Through you a phaser

Awesome is game

Protect that space

Password through the web

I rule and figure

Non-Apparent

Do I talk A lot?

Maybe so.

Do I wish for a lot?

Maybe so.

Do I love it too quickly?

Maybe so.

Do I miss them much?

Maybe so.

Hero

Your the hero in your own story

And the villain in another one.

It's all up to you who wins in both worlds

And loses in others.

Babe

With a swing at the bat

And the base getting wider,

His hat's looking quite fat

And his whole world is getting higher.

His opinion is quite stern

And the drawing is huge.

It shall not be burned

While all his words are muse.

Babe is a real catch

Whom the artist wishes for gold.

Babe and his bat are a real catch

But his story is way too big to unfold.

The Fun and Happy Depression

Whose depression Is that? I think I know

It's owner is quite sad however.

It really is a tale of woe

As we all watch him frown, Let's give him a jolly old hello.

He gives his depression a shake

Just to make sure that it's still awake.

The only other sounds that break

Are the distant waves and birds that awake.

The man's depression is fun, happy and gleeful

One might even say that to him it's helpful.

Until it ends he shall not sleep

As he lies in bed waiting for his ends to finally meet.

As he rises from his bitter bed

With thoughts of sadness in his head.

He idolizes the day that this all will end

Facing the inevitable return of his ongoing dread.

THE FUN AND HAPPY DEPRESSION

Jazz Night

Don't let the night die out like this

Have fun a little in the moonlight.

Drop down and ride the night like a wave at full pace

You'll just might find the love of your life.

Come over and dance to some sweet jazz

While you let go of life's problems and ride free.

Just don't lag with all the stress and lingering

THE FUN AND HAPPY DEPRESSION

Do you really think that i'll let you go without proper lighting?

Rio

Enjoy the smog breeze

And the coffee on the swerving counter.

Come take a sweet drive with me

But the move can't go any faster.

The wind takes my breath away

While we pop open a fresh glass of wine.

You can try to drink the night away

But only after we're done basking in the beautiful trees

Bask in the amazing scenery

And the magnificent culture.

But you've got to ask yourself however

Is it all enough to love?

Homie Love

My love for my brother will go on forever and ever

When he's the only one who could keep it together.

Everytime that I someone would fall, he would be at their rescue

Even when he knew that his passion would not last forever.

Fable

With one big and grand wish

The little boy was grinning for a hot meal.

The boy knew all of his risks

Yet he even balled up his fists.

When the boy didn't get what he wanted

He wished up a big storm for all the ages.

One that would wipe out all the villages for miles away

And would bring his whole world down for ages.

"No young lad, that's not how it works."

Said the little boy's mother.

"You can't just destroy things just to get what you want."

The little boy felt ashamed and embarrassed at his behavior.

When the boy put everything back to normal

His mother gave him the meal he wanted.

Let's just hope that he doesn't wish for more.

THE FUN AND HAPPY DEPRESSION

Blackout Poem 1

I told him why the night counts

When he asked why it mattered.

It is a rather concerning question

On the idea of being a pattern.

THE FUN AND HAPPY DEPRESSION

Don't miss out!

Visit the website below and you can sign up to receive emails whenever Jay Ocean publishes a new book. There's no charge and no obligation.

https://books2read.com/r/B-A-XNFN-LQKIB

BOOKS 2 READ

Connecting independent readers to independent writers.

Did you love *The Fun and Happy Depression*? Then you should read *The Girl With The Bloody Nose*[1] by Jay Ocean and Rebecka Hennis!

[2]

"The Girl With The Bloody Nose" is a collection of 10 poems that all horror fans will love. It tackles the mind of wicked things in the land of sorrow and misery.

---

1. https://books2read.com/u/mvnx0V

2. https://books2read.com/u/mvnx0V

Also by Jay Ocean

The Fun and Happy Depression
The Girl With The Bloody Nose

Watch for more at https://www.instagram.com/jayguyman/.

About the Author

"Jay Ocean" was born in Ripley Mississippi and was born to be a poet. From a young age, he loved to tell stories that entertained people and captures their imaginations. Besides being a poet, he is also a model, actor and podcaster.

Read more at https://www.instagram.com/jayguyman/.

www.ingramcontent.com/pod-product-compliance
Lightning Source LLC
Chambersburg PA
CBHW061432050726
47593CB00006B/2327